CATS & KITTENS
Drawing & Activity Book

Brimming with creative inspiration, how-to projects, and useful information to enrich your everyday life, Quarto Knows is a favorite destination for those pursuing their interests and passions. Visit our site and dig deeper with our books into your area of interest: Quarto Creates, Quarto Cooks, Quarto Homes, Quarto Lives, Quarto Drives, Quarto Explores, Quarto Gifts, or Quarto Kids.

© 2005, 2014, 2019 Quarto Publishing Group USA Inc.
Photographs © Shutterstock

First published in 2019 by Walter Foster Jr., an imprint of The Quarto Group. 26391 Crown Valley Parkway, Suite 220, Mission Viejo, CA, USA.
T (949) 380-7510 F (949) 380-7575 www.QuartoKnows.com

All rights reserved. No part of this book may be reproduced in any form without written permission of the copyright owners. All images in this book have been reproduced with the knowledge and prior consent of the artists concerned, and no responsibility is accepted by producer, publisher, or printer for any infringement of copyright or otherwise, arising from the contents of this publication. Every effort has been made to ensure that credits accurately comply with information supplied. We apologize for any inaccuracies that may have occurred and will resolve inaccurate or missing information in a subsequent reprinting of the book.

Walter Foster Jr. titles are also available at discount for retail, wholesale, promotional, and bulk purchase. For details, contact the Special Sales Manager by email at specialsales@quarto.com or by mail at The Quarto Group, Attn: Special Sales Manager, 100 Cummings Center, Suite 265D, Beverly, MA 01915, USA.

ISBN: 978-1-63322-703-3

Illustrated by Robbin Cuddy and Diana Fisher.

Printed in China
10 9 8 7 6 5 4 3 2

TABLE OF CONTENTS

Tools & Materials 4
Tracing Basics 5
Grid Method 6
Step-by-Step Method 7
Persian Kitten 8
Russian Blue 10
Maine Coon 12
Cat Breed Word Search 16
Mouser Maze 17
Siamese 18
Scottish Fold 20
Bengal 22
Selkirk Rex Kitten 26
Ragdoll 28
Abyssinian Kitten 30
Hidden Kitty Follow the Numbers 34
Cat Facts Mini Quiz 35
Egyptian Mau 36
Birman 38
British Shorthair 40
Spot the Differences 44
Cracking the Cat Code 45
Turkish Angora 46
Sphynx 50
Himalayan Kitten 52
All Grown Up! 56
9 Lives Sudoku 57
Norwegian Forest Cats 58
Siberian 60
Answers 64

TOOLS & MATERIALS

You need to gather only a few simple art supplies before you begin. Start with a drawing pencil and an eraser. Make sure you also have a pencil sharpener! Finish your drawings using your choice of art supplies pictured below, such as markers or paints.

drawing pencil

pencils

felt-tip markers

crayons

sharpener

drawing paper

eraser

paintbrushes

paints

TRACING BASICS

This book has five sheets of blank tracing paper, which you can use to trace the cat pictured on the pages after them.

tracing paper

Trace your own Egyptian Mau on the transparent paper!

With your pencil, draw everything you can see over the cat you're tracing, paying close attention to all the little details. Lift the tracing paper up to see your progress.

GRID METHOD

When using the grid method, don't worry about the drawing as a whole. Focus on copying the lines and shapes of just one small square at a time.

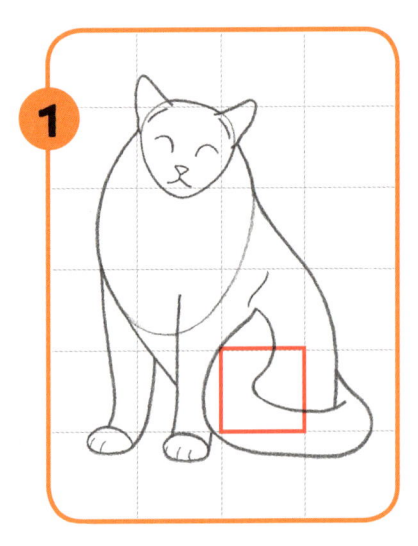

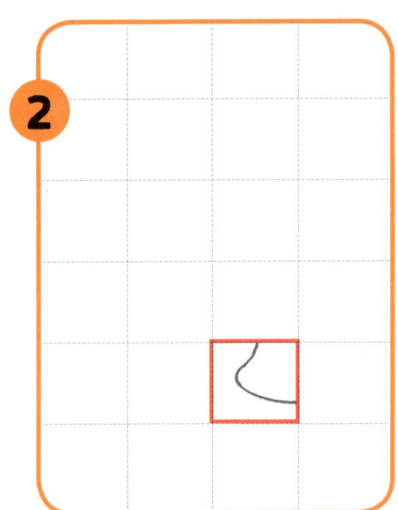

Choose a square and copy everything into the same square on your blank grid. Make sure you are copying the shapes and lines into the correct spot!

After you've completed all the squares in step one, move on to the next step and keep going!

STEP-BY-STEP METHOD

When using the step-by-step drawing method, you will begin by drawing very basic shapes, such as lines and circles. Each cat with step-by-step instructions has a blank page for you to draw on.

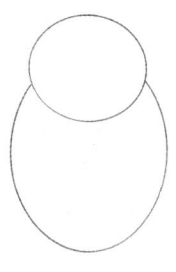

1
First draw the basic shapes, using light lines that will be easy to erase.

2
Pay attention to the new lines added in each step.

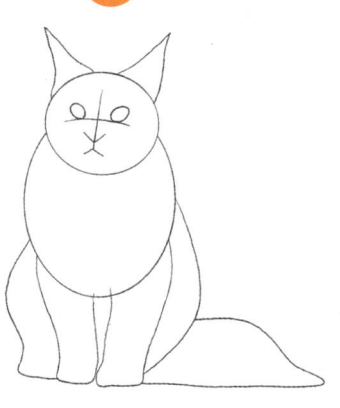

3
Add more defining lines with each new step.

4
Erase guidelines and add more detail.

5
Take your time adding detail and copying what you see.

6
Finish your drawing with pencils, markers, paints, or crayons!

Tracing Method

PERSIAN KITTEN

The Persian cat may seem hoity-toity, but other than making sure its fur stays brushed and clean, this breed is low-maintenance.

FUN FACT
The Persian's characteristic flat face came from a genetic mutation, which breeders liked. There are still traditional Persians, which have a pointier muzzle.

Trace your own Persian kitten on the transparent paper!

Grid Method

RUSSIAN BLUE

Quiet-loving Blues can happily sit still for hours.

FUN FACT
This shy breed is gentle, shy, and likes to watch what's going on from high places. But once a Blue is comfortable with you, it will always be by your side.

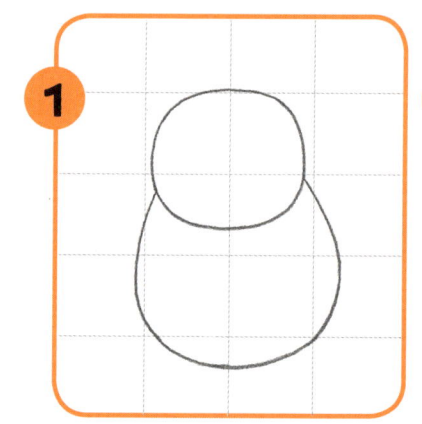

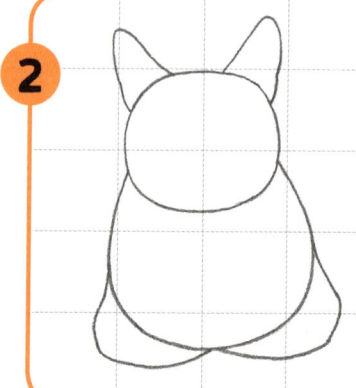

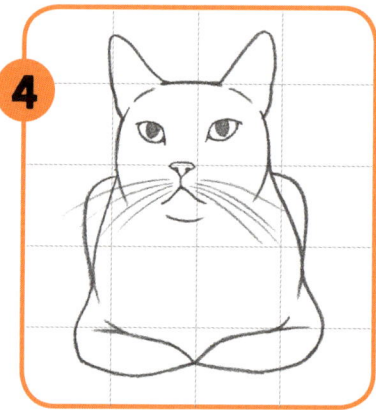

1
2
3
4
5

10

Copy the lines shown in each step. When you're done with all the steps, you'll have a complete drawing of a Russian Blue. Add details to your drawing with markers, pencils, crayons, or paints.

Step-by-Step

MAINE COON

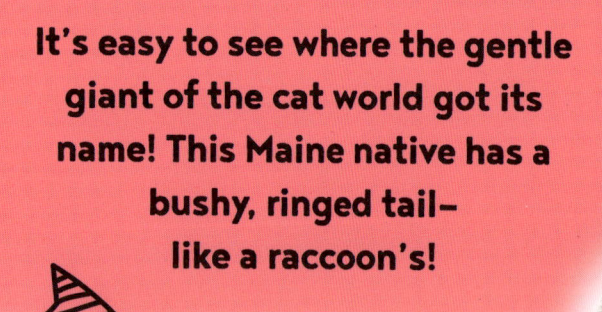

It's easy to see where the gentle giant of the cat world got its name! This Maine native has a bushy, ringed tail—like a raccoon's!

FUN FACT
Maine Coons can use their large front paws to open doors!

Follow along, first drawing basic shapes with light pencil lines. Copy the new lines shown in each step, eventually darkening the lines you want to keep and erasing the rest. Finally add details to your drawing with pencils, markers, paints, or crayons.

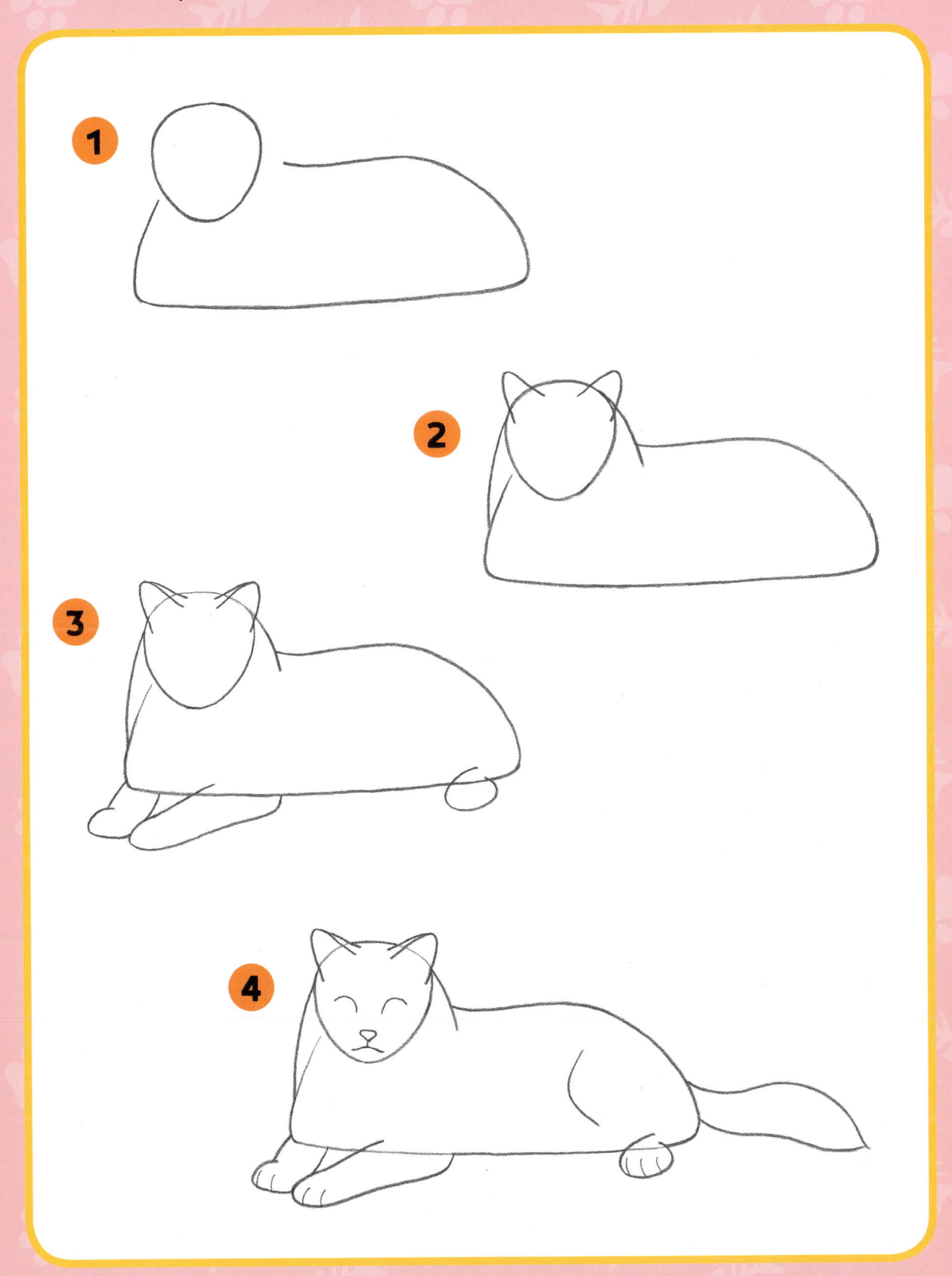

1
2
3
4

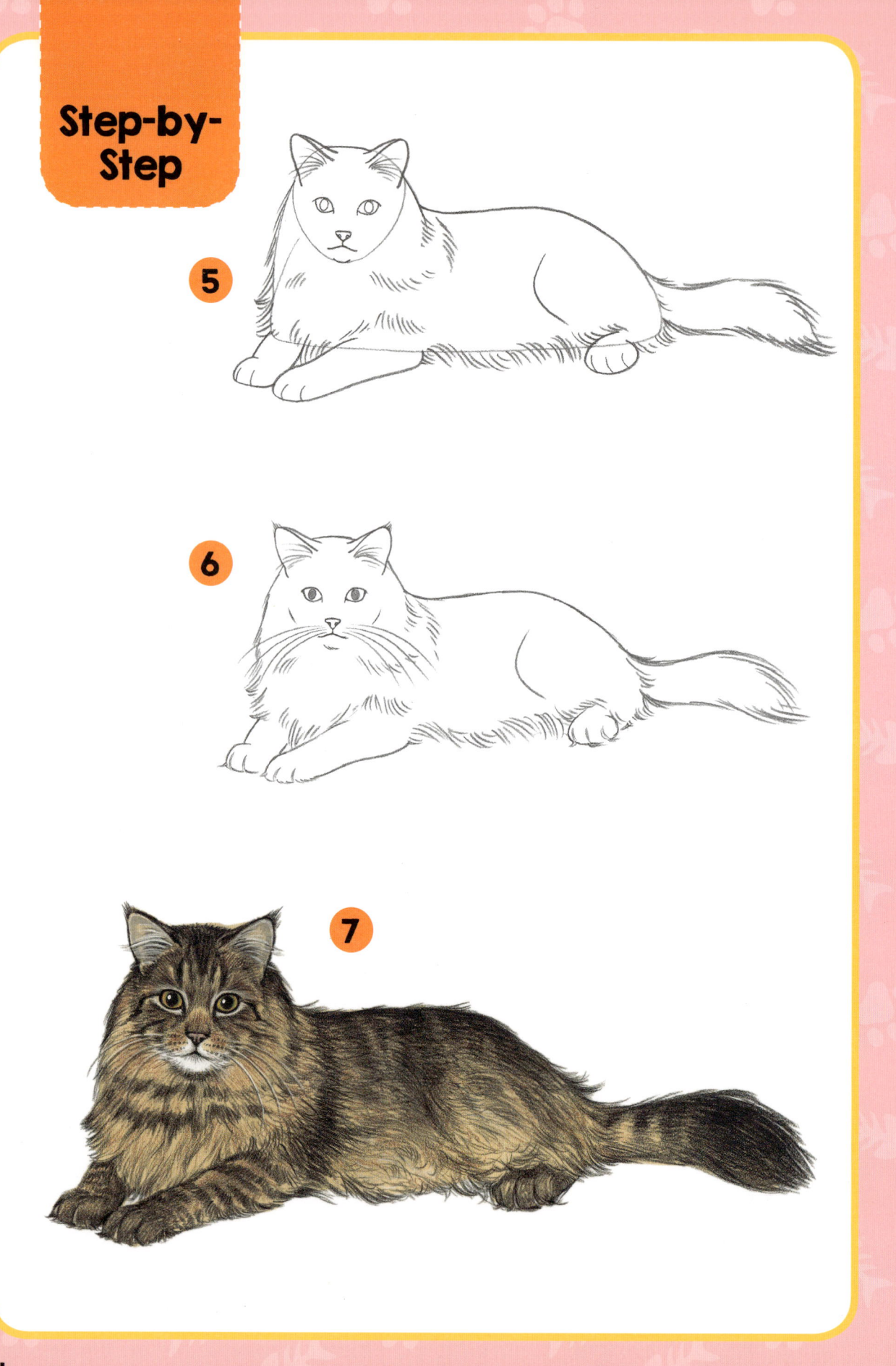

Step-by-Step

5

6

7

14

Draw your own Maine Coon here!

CAT BREED WORD SEARCH

Find and circle the names of different cat breeds hidden in the letters below.

```
G Z P E R S I A N E X T I X O X Q F A I
H A K A E Q N U N K O R A T J D V R J B
F O N F J E N L A O C I C A T A O C K F
M O D R A G D O L L J L U O P G E M S I
H A V A N A B R O W N R D R N E Z E S H
I Y E T J V R F F D Q V N A R N R G C W
T S Z Y M A N X H E R E H I U W B Y O P
Z L L I S J J B S Y N S F H S M R P T S
N X A X F G X E A O I J V S S A B T T R
L W B Z W L M T B K Y A A E I I E I I L
N V Y R N R M L R L T V H D A N N A S U
V S S K U V G U C C V A A W N E G N H Z
S I S B S M T R J U Y N U D B C A M F M
W A I O J Y O H B T C E Y F L O L A O R
I M N X R T R M G C A S A I U O R U L P
F E I K C U T C A Z X E O Z E N W F D D
R S A H B K U B I P C H A R T R E U X P
H E N E X O T I C S H O R T H A I R W F
```

- ☐ Abyssinian
- ☐ Chartreux
- ☐ Havana Brown
- ☐ Maine Coon
- ☐ Persian
- ☐ Scottish Fold
- ☐ Bengal
- ☐ Egyptian Mau
- ☐ Javanese
- ☐ Manx
- ☐ Ragdoll
- ☐ Siamese
- ☐ Burmese
- ☐ Exotic Shorthair
- ☐ Korat
- ☐ Ocicat
- ☐ Russian Blue
- ☐ Turkish Angora

Answers on page 64.

MOUSER MAZE

Help kitty find her way to the toy mouse!

START

FINISH

17

Answers on page 64.

Tracing Method

SIAMESE

Siamese are talkative cats, and their voices sometimes sound like a crying child.

FUN FACT

Siamese kittens are born all white. The dark "points" on their tails, paws, ears, and faces only develop on cooler parts of the body, not their warm torsos.

Trace your own Siamese on the transparent paper!

Grid Method

SCOTTISH FOLD

This affectionate breed is known for its folded ears, which give it an owl-like appearance.

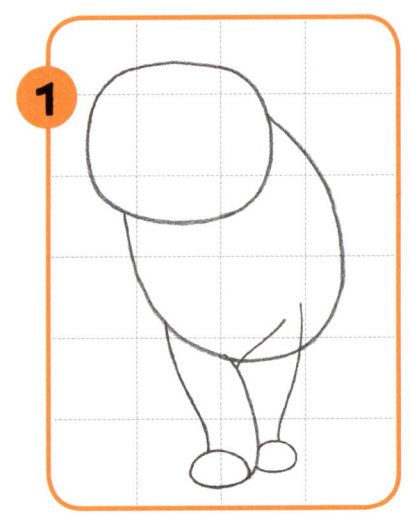

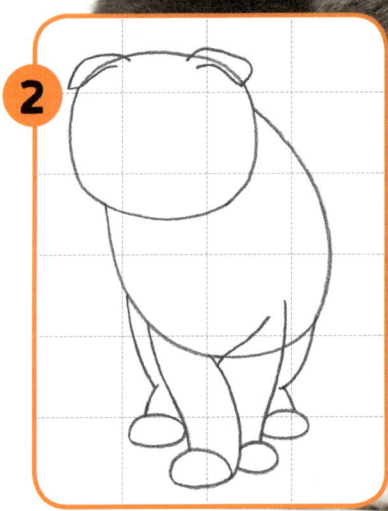

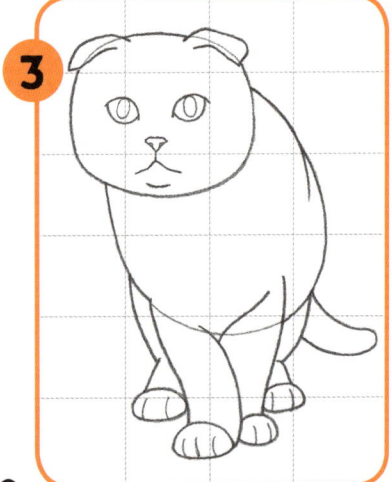

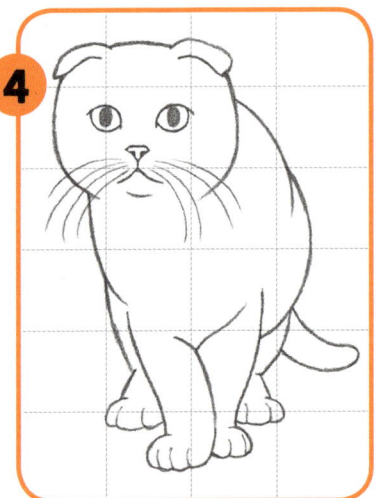

Copy the lines shown in each step. When you're done with all the steps, you'll have a complete drawing of a Scottish Fold. Add details to your drawing with markers, pencils, crayons, or paints.

21

Step-by-Step

BENGAL

These highly intelligent cats are active and agile and demand a lot of attention.

FUN FACT
Bengals love to play in water!

Follow along, first drawing basic shapes with light pencil lines. Copy the new lines shown in each step, eventually darkening the lines you want to keep and erasing the rest. Finally add details to your drawing with pencils, markers, paints, or crayons.

23

Step-by-Step

4

5

24

Draw your own Bengal here!

Tracing Method

SELKIRK REX

Selkirk Rex kittens often have shaggy, rumpled-looking fur. When they reach adulthood, their wavy locks become curly coats.

FUN FACT
Like the Cornish Rex and the Devon Rex, the Selkirk Rex has a curly coat. But with its stronger, rounder body, it looks very different from its fellow "Rex" cats.

Trace your own Selkirk Rex on the transparent paper!

Grid Method

RAGDOLL

This soft, fluffy cat is so relaxed that it flops like a rag doll when picked up! An affectionate breed, Ragdolls love to cuddle.

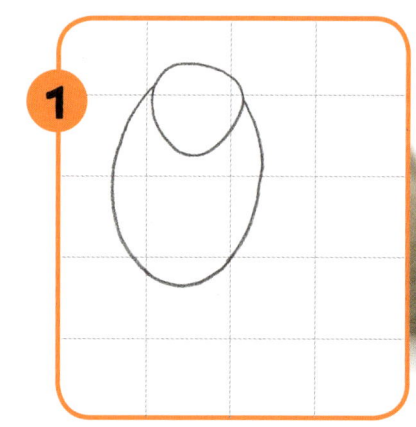

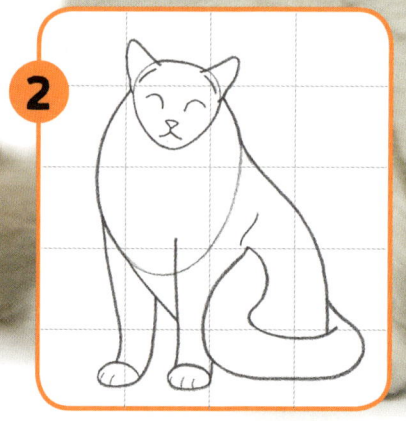

1
2
3
4
5

Copy the lines shown in each step. When you're done with all the steps, you'll have a complete drawing of a Ragdoll. Add details to your drawing with markers, pencils, crayons, or paints.

29

Step-by-Step

ABYSSINIAN KITTEN

Abyssinians are cats with short hair and strong bodies—and stronger personalities! These curious kitties are intelligent and outgoing.

FUN FACT
This athletic feline can jump up to 6 feet (2 m) in the air!

Follow along, first drawing basic shapes with light pencil lines. Copy the new lines shown in each step, eventually darkening the lines you want to keep and erasing the rest. Finally add details to your drawing with pencils, markers, paints, or crayons.

31

Step-by-Step

5

6

7

8

32

Draw your own Abyssinian kitten here!

HIDDEN KITTY FOLLOW THE NUMBERS

Fill in each numbered space with a matching shade from the guide below to reveal the hidden picture.

- 1 (black)
- 2 (green)
- 3 (brown)
- 4 (orange)
- 5 (peach)

2	2	2	2	2	2	2	2	2	2	2
2	2	4	2	2	2	2	2	4	2	2
2	2	5	4	2	2	2	4	5	2	2
2	5	5	4	3	4	3	4	5	5	2
2	5	4	4	3	4	3	4	4	5	2
2	4	4	4	4	4	4	4	4	4	2
2	3	4	1	4	4	4	1	4	3	2
2	4	4	4		1		4	4	4	2
2	3	4	4				4	4	3	2
2	2	2	4	4	4	4	4	2	2	2
2	2	2	2	2	2	2	2	2	2	2

34

Answers on page 64.

CAT FACTS MINI QUIZ

1. True or false? The British Shorthair's coat has more fur per square inch (cm) than any other cat breed.

2. How fast can an Egyptian Mau run?
   A. 15 miles (24 km) per hour
   B. 22 miles (32 km) per hour
   C. 30 miles (48 km) per hour
   D. 50 miles (80 km) per hour

3. The Himalayan is a mix between what two breeds?
   A. Siamese and Persians
   B. Ragdolls and Persians
   C. Ragdolls and Siamese
   D. Maine Coon and Siamese

4. A Norwegian Forest Cat's eyes can be:
   A. Green
   B. Gold
   C. Copper
   D. Any of the above

5. True or false? Persians have the longest and thickest fur of all domestic cats.

6. How far back can the modern Siamese trace its ancestors?
   A. 12th century
   B. 14th century
   C. 18th century
   D. 20th century

Answers on page 64.

35

Tracing Method

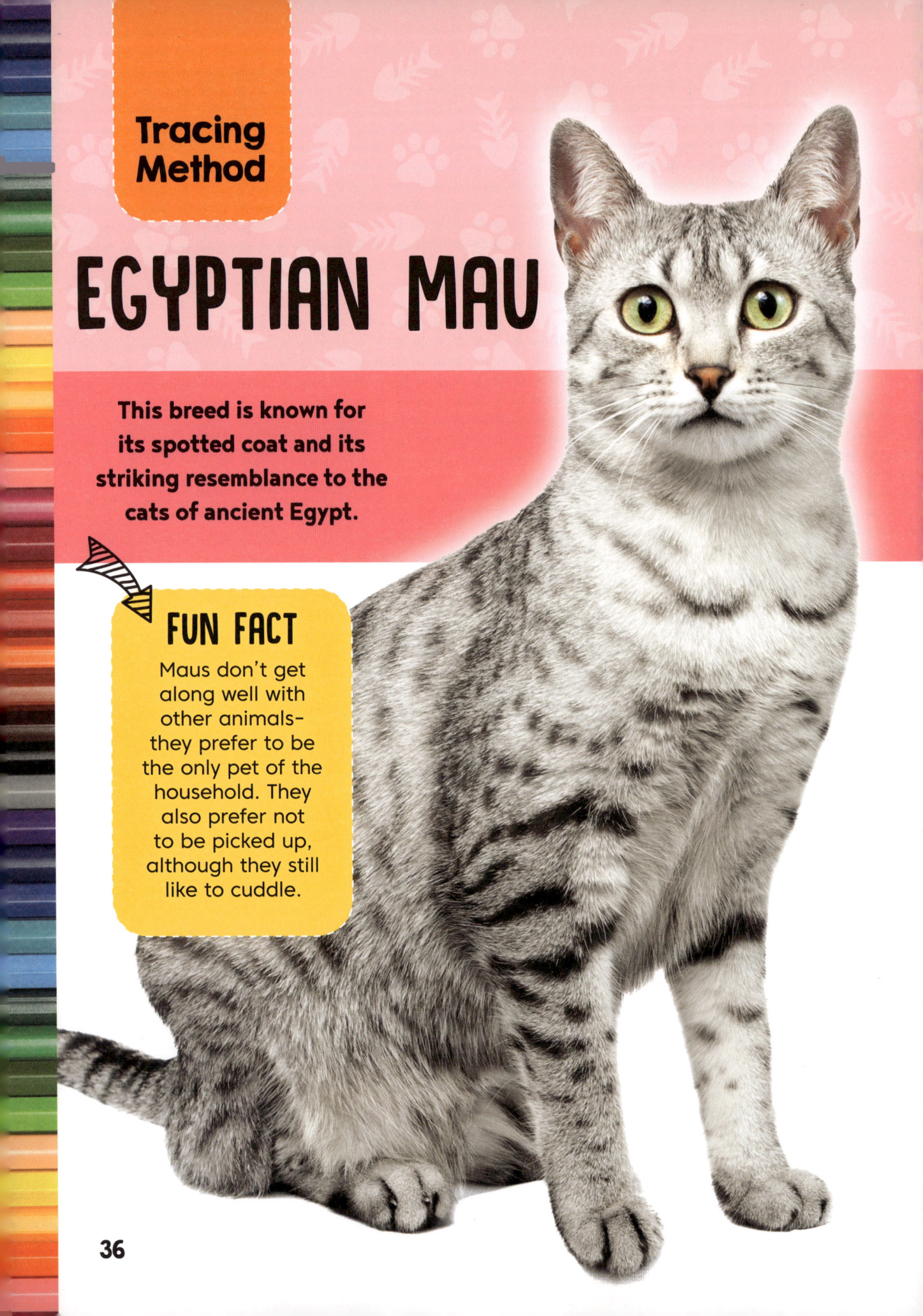

EGYPTIAN MAU

This breed is known for its spotted coat and its striking resemblance to the cats of ancient Egypt.

FUN FACT

Maus don't get along well with other animals—they prefer to be the only pet of the household. They also prefer not to be picked up, although they still like to cuddle.

Trace your own Egyptian Mau on the transparent paper!

Grid Method

BIRMAN

The round white paws on this breed—also known as "The Sacred Cat of Burma"—distinguish it from other breeds with the same markings.

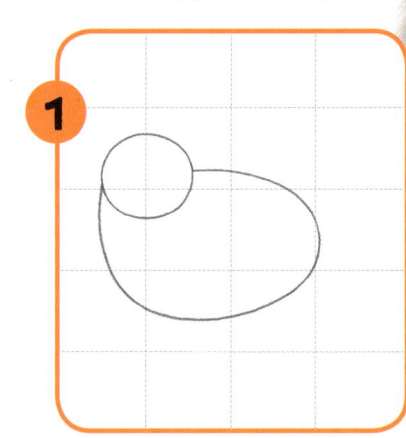

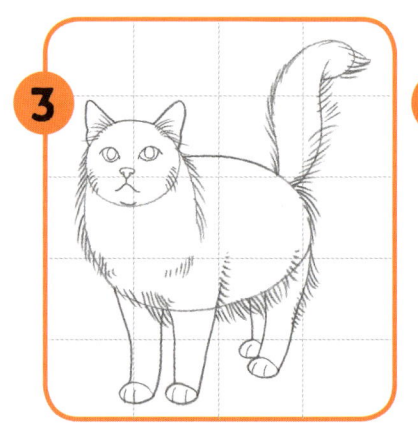

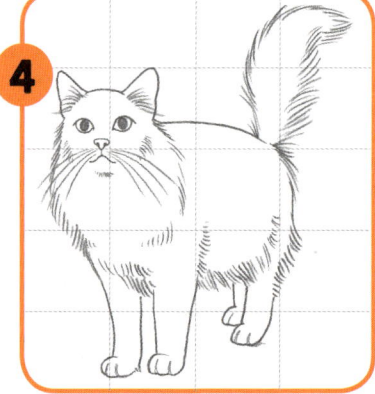

1
2
3
4
5

Copy the lines shown in each step. When you're done with all the steps, you'll have a complete drawing of a Birman kitten. Add details to your drawing with markers, pencils, crayons, or paints.

BRITISH SHORTHAIR

Step-by-Step

This large and lazy lap cat loves affection and doesn't make much noise.

FUN FACT
British Shorthairs are usually "blue" (which doesn't really look blue), but they come in a variety of patterns.

40

Follow along, first drawing basic shapes with light pencil lines. Copy the new lines shown in each step, eventually darkening the lines you want to keep and erasing the rest. Finally add details to your drawing with pencils, markers, paints, or crayons.

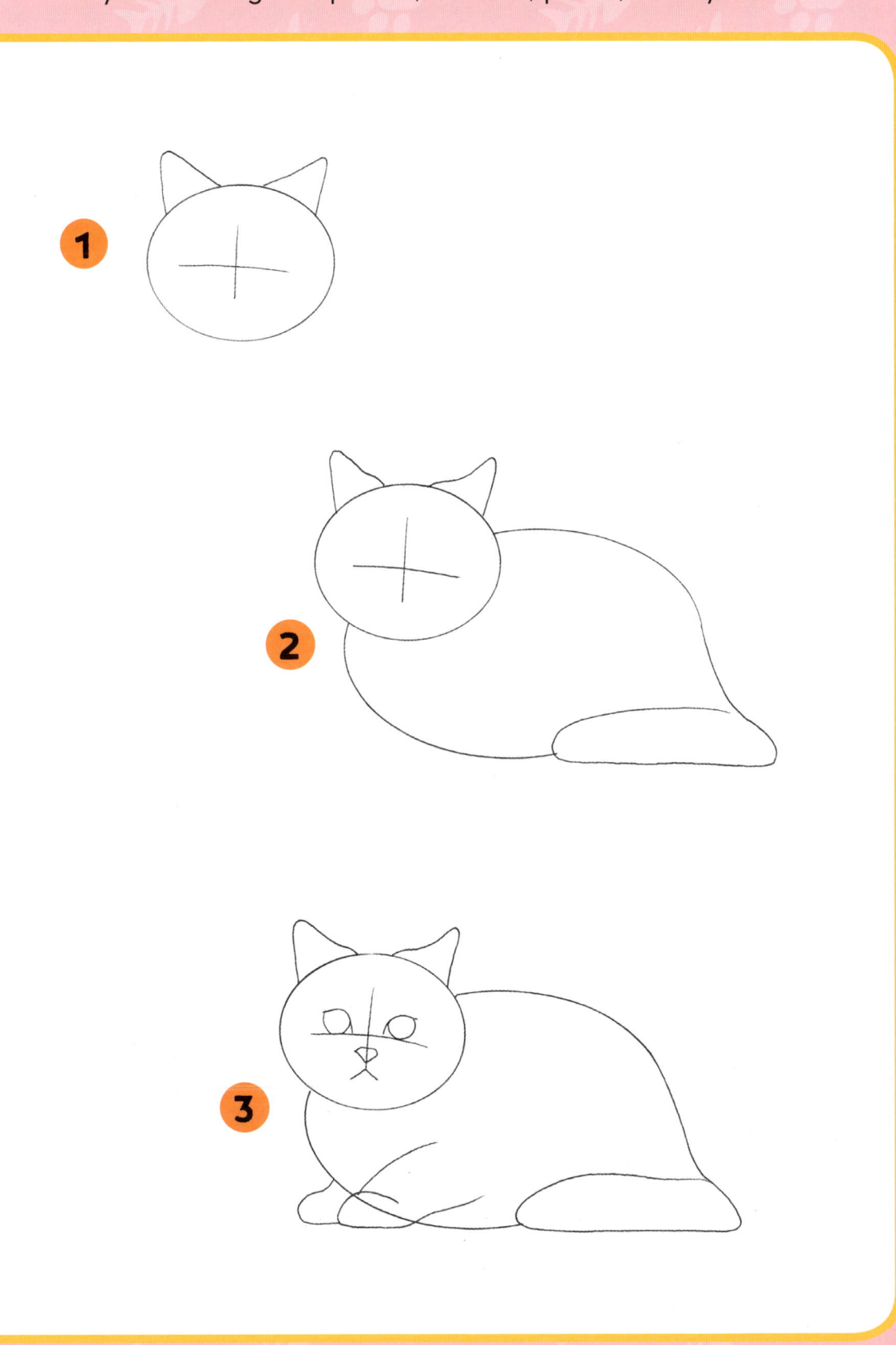

1

2

3

41

Step-by-Step

4

5

6

42

Draw your own British Shorthair here!

SPOT THE DIFFERENCES

Can you spot six differences between these two photos?

Answers on page 64.

44

CRACKING THE CAT CODE

Use the code to find out an awesome cat fact.
The letters are missing. Can you crack the code?

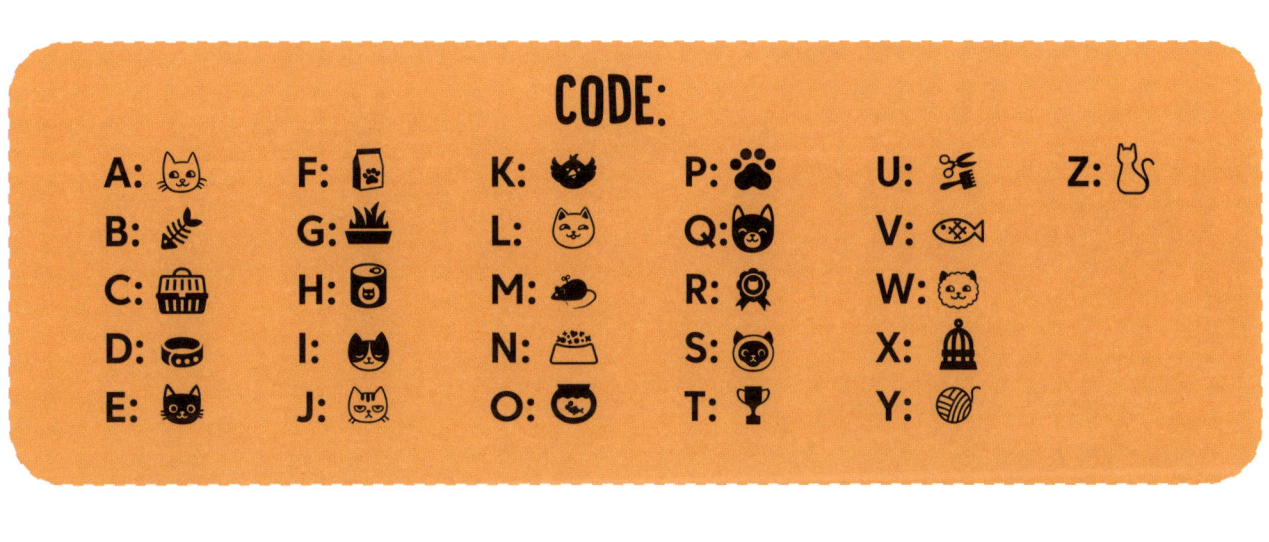

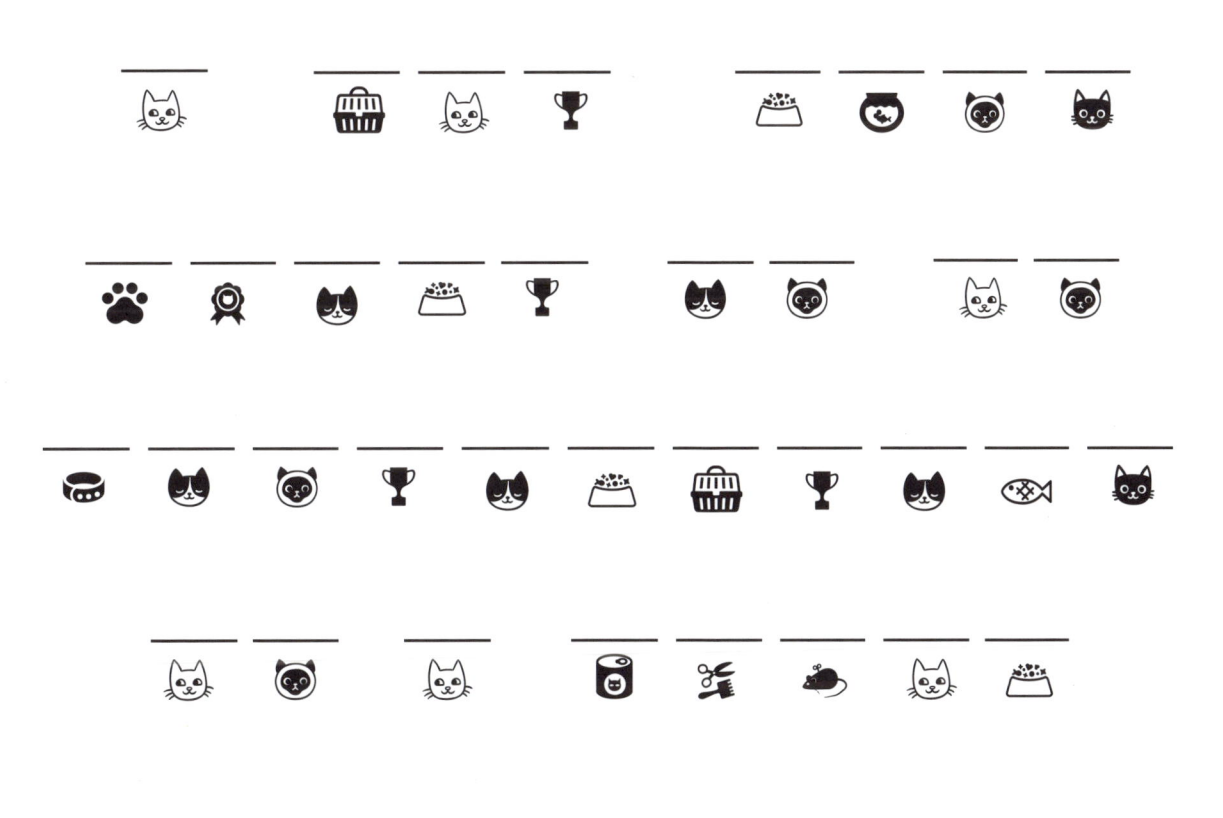

CODE:

A: 🐱 F: 🐟 K: 🐱 P: 🐾 U: ✂️ Z: 🐈
B: 🐟 G: 🌱 L: 😺 Q: 🐶 V: 🐟
C: 🧺 H: 🥫 M: 🐭 R: 🏅 W: 🐱
D: 🦴 I: 😼 N: 🍲 S: 😺 X: 🏺
E: 🐱 J: 😾 O: 🐟 T: 🏆 Y: 🧶

Answers on page 64.

45

Step-by-Step

TURKISH ANGORA

The luxurious-looking Turkish Angora is clever, athletic, and needs to be played with often.

FUN FACT

Turkish Angoras are well known for their long, majestic white fur and having one blue eye and one amber eye.

Follow along, first drawing basic shapes with light pencil lines. Copy the new lines shown in each step, eventually darkening the lines you want to keep and erasing the rest. Finally add details to your drawing with pencils, markers, paints, or crayons.

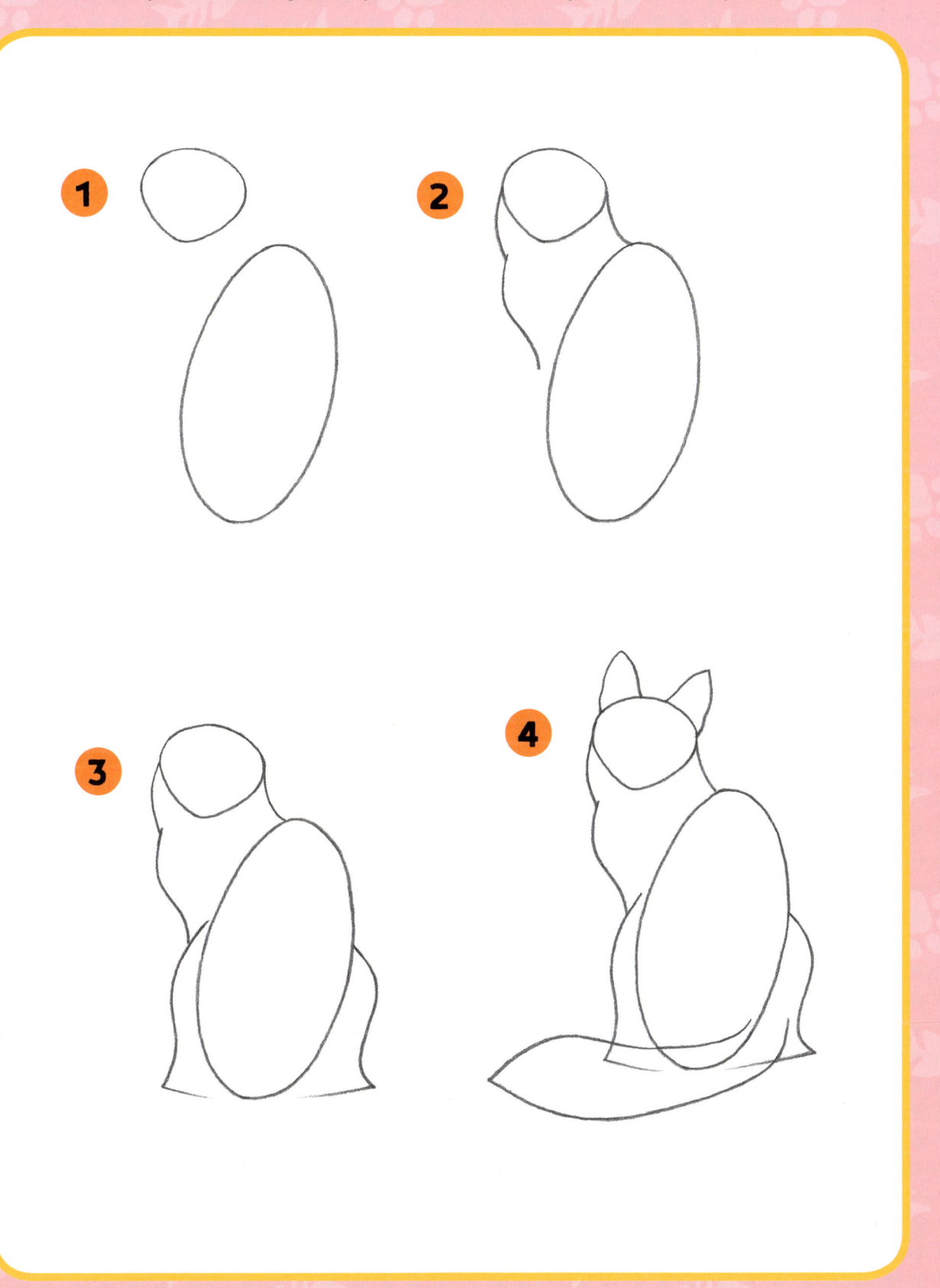

47

Step-by-Step

5

6

7

8

48

Draw your own Turkish Angora here!

Tracing Method

SPHYNX

The huge, triangular ears of this hairless cat are hard to miss! And its wrinkled skin, wide-set eyes, and large paws also draw attention.

FUN FACT

Although it is referred to as "hairless," the Sphynx does have a very fine covering of fur, especially on the ears, face, feet, and tail.

Use the transparent paper to make your own Sphynx!

51

Step-by-Step

HIMALAYAN KITTEN

These stocky, longhaired cats are shy and prefer a calm, quiet home. They become attached to their humans and love to sit in their laps.

FUN FACT

Himalayans look just like Persian cats, except they have the eyes and markings of a Siamese. Why is that? Breeders created this breed using Persian and Siamese cats!

Follow along, first drawing basic shapes with light pencil lines. Copy the new lines shown in each step, eventually darkening the lines you want to keep and erasing the rest. Finally add details to your drawing with pencils, markers, paints, or crayons.

1.

2.

3.

Step-by-Step

4

5

Draw your own Himalayan kitten here!

ALL GROWN UP!

Match the breed! Draw a line to connect each kitten to the adult cat of the same breed.

56

Answers on page 64.

9 LIVES SUDOKU

Solve the sudoku puzzle by filling in the blanks using the numbers 1-9. Each number can only be used one time in a row, column, and box.

2			5		1	4		
	3		8			6		
8		1		7				
		6			3	9		5
4			1		7		2	
	5				9			8
	8		6					1
6				3	2		9	
	7						5	2

Answers on page 64.

Grid Method

NORWEGIAN FOREST CATS

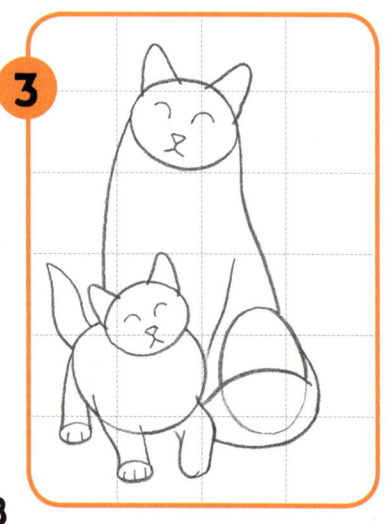

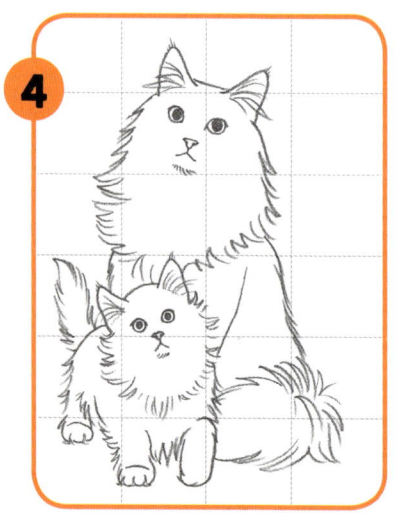

This furry feline has a thick, heavy coat of fur. Its mane and tail are fluffy, and its triangular ears are straight and tall!

1.
2.
3.
4.
5.

Copy the lines shown in each step. When you're done with all the steps, you'll have a complete drawing of the cats. Add details to your drawing with markers, pencils, crayons, or paints.

Step-by-Step

SIBERIAN

This gentle giant is devoted to its owners and good with children and other pets.

FUN FACT

People believe this breed is hypoallergenic, meaning that if you are allergic to cats, this breed might not make you sneeze!

Follow along, first drawing basic shapes with light pencil lines. Copy the new lines shown in each step, eventually darkening the lines you want to keep and erasing the rest. Finally add details to your drawing with pencils, markers, paints, or crayons.

61

Step-by-Step

4

5

6

62

Draw your own Siberian here!

ANSWERS

Page 16: Cat Breed Word Search

Page 17: Mouser Maze

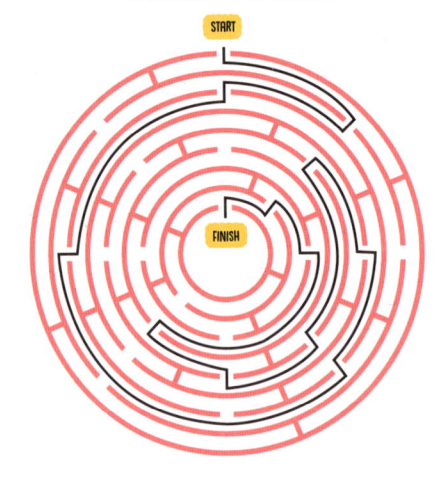

Page 34: Hidden Kitty Follow the Numbers

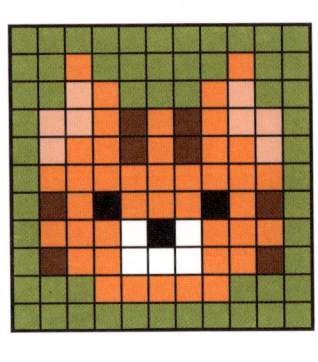

Page 35: Cat Facts Mini Quiz

1. True! The British Shorthair's coat is the most dense of any breed. Its has a plush texture, not really woolly or fluffy.
2. C. The Egyptian Mau is the fastest cat breed and can run up to 30 miles (50 km) an hour.
3. A. Cat breeders wanted a Persian cat with the pattern of the Siamese, so they used these two breeds to create the Himalayan.
4. D. Any of the above. You can find Norwegian Forest Cats with all kinds of eye shades.
5. True! A Persian's fur can grow up to 5 inches (13 cm) in length! Persians require daily grooming in order to keep their fur from matting.
6. B. The Siamese traces its royal roots all the way back to the 14th century in Thailand, when it was called Siam.

Page 44: Spot the Differences

Page 45: Cracking the Cat Code

A cat nose print is as distinctive as a human fingerprint.

Page 56: All Grown Up!

Page 57: 9 Lives Sudoku

2	6	7	5	9	1	4	8	3
5	3	9	8	2	4	6	1	7
8	4	1	3	7	6	2	5	9
1	2	6	4	8	3	9	7	5
4	9	8	1	5	7	3	2	6
7	5	3	2	6	9	1	4	8
9	8	2	6	4	5	7	3	1
6	1	5	7	3	2	8	9	4
3	7	4	9	1	8	5	6	2